Simply Stunning
Seamless Quilts

14 EASY PROJECTS TO FUSE

Anna Faustino

 **PUBLISHING**

Text copyright © 2015 by Anna Faustino

Photography and artwork copyright © 2015 by C&T Publishing, Inc.

Publisher: Amy Marson

Creative Director: Gailen Runge

Art Director: Kristy Zacharias

Editor: Liz Aneloski

Technical Editors: Nan Powell and Mary E. Flynn

Cover Designers: Christina Jarumay Fox and April Mostek

Book Designer: Christina Jarumay Fox

Production Coordinators: Jenny Davis and Zinnia Heinzmann

Production Editor: Alice Mace Nakanishi

Photo Assistant: Mary Peyton Peppo

Photography by Diane Pedersen, unless otherwise noted

Published by C&T Publishing, Inc., P.O. Box 1456, Lafayette, CA 94549

Library of Congress Cataloging-in-Publication Data

Faustino, Anna, 1955-

  Simply stunning seamless quilts : 14 easy projects to fuse / Anna Faustino.

    pages cm

  Includes bibliographical references.

  ISBN 978-1-61745-022-8 (soft cover)

  1. Patchwork quilts. 2. Patchwork--Patterns. 3. Quilting--Patterns. 4. Fusible materials in sewing. I. Title.

  TT835.F3778 2015

  746.46--dc23

                    2015010888

Printed in China

10 9 8 7 6 5 4 3 2 1

Contents

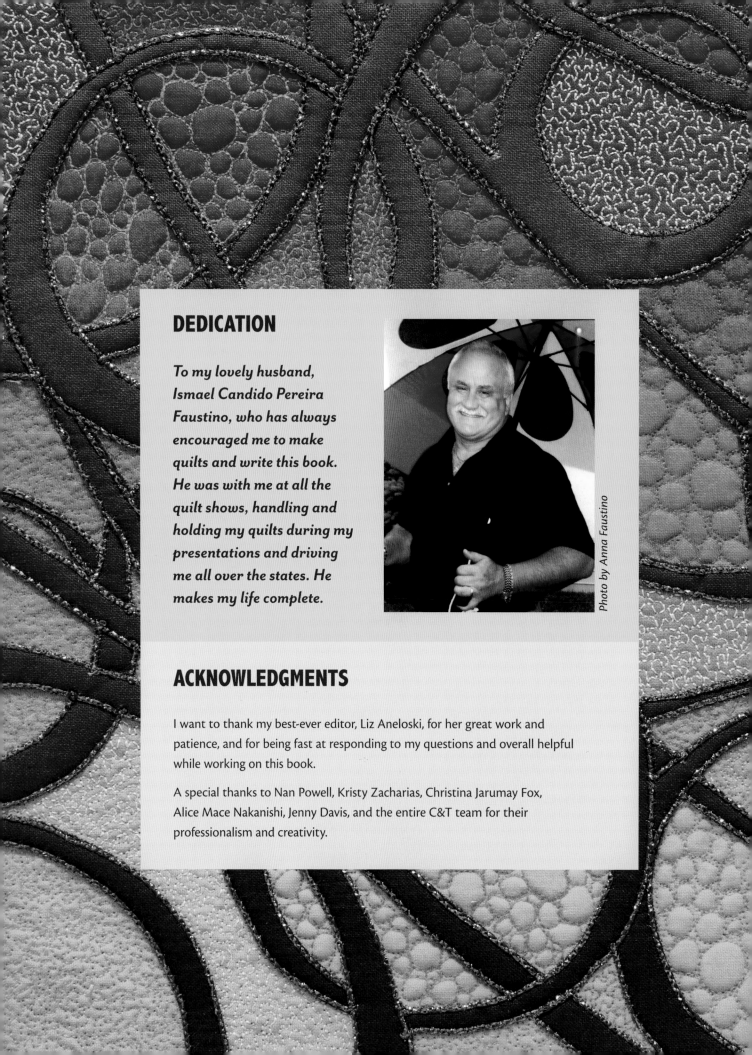

DEDICATION

To my lovely husband, Ismael Candido Pereira Faustino, who has always encouraged me to make quilts and write this book. He was with me at all the quilt shows, handling and holding my quilts during my presentations and driving me all over the states. He makes my life complete.

Photo by Anna Faustino

ACKNOWLEDGMENTS

I want to thank my best-ever editor, Liz Aneloski, for her great work and patience, and for being fast at responding to my questions and overall helpful while working on this book.

A special thanks to Nan Powell, Kristy Zacharias, Christina Jarumay Fox, Alice Mace Nakanishi, Jenny Davis, and the entire C&T team for their professionalism and creativity.

Foreword

I learned to use textiles and create art by experimenting and just doing. The journey since my first book, *Simply Stunning Woven Quilts,* has been like navigating my way through a labyrinth and into an absolutely unexpected direction in textile art. I'm anxious to share this new direction with you.

I hope you will embrace the ideas in this book and allow it to lead you on a creative adventure. As you work your way through the book, whether you are a beginning or experienced quilter, I hope you are excited and inspired by the quilts, the projects, and this wonderful technique and that it leads to an unending supply of ideas for future quilts.

The exciting secret is that you get to be responsible for the choices: design, color, fabric, embellishments, and finishing. It can be a little frightening, but so exhilarating. That's a big part of the creativity. It's all up to you. There are no limits.

I love creative work. Let it be so!

Introduction

WHAT IS AN OUTLINE DESIGN?

An Outline Design is made up of lines in a variety of widths that form shapes. After the design is cut out of a prefused wholecloth surface (raw-edge appliqué style), the shapes of the openings are filled with one or more different fabrics. The Outline Design inspiration can be abstract or representational.

This bold and simple technique, shown in the projects and inspiration quilts throughout the book, has endless possibilities. It is a cross between putting together a puzzle and painting by number. Follow one of the projects, step by step, or create your own original design; anybody who can create

a doodle or line drawing can create or adapt almost any design into an original quilt. This book will help you to find new and exciting ways to create artistic, original quilts. Explore portraits, still life, landscapes, traditional-style quilts, even crazy quilts.

The cutting method for this technique is to freehand cut with a craft knife. This tool is easy and comfortable to use if you are familiar with the rotary cutter. After a couple hours of practice you will be a professional. Each project includes an Outline Design pattern; some will need to be enlarged, but there are two full-size patterns on the pattern pullout page that are ready to trace. This technique allows us to cut the very detailed, delicate elements of the Outline Designs, creating perfect curves, circles, and intersections.

Here are a few benefits of the Outline Design technique:

- These quilts have no piecing or seams.

- There are no hand stitches or turned-under edges.

- The Outline Design can be any color or print and lines can be a variety of widths.

- You can audition and change the fabrics that fill the openings between the Outline Design and the background fabric or directly onto prefused batting many times before permanently fusing them in place.

- You can save the cutout pieces from cutting out the Design Outline to make a second quilt in a reverse value negative image (see *Butterfly Garden*, page 25, and *Night Butterfly*, page 29, as examples).

- The design possibilities are endless.

Please consider personalizing the projects. If you try by making small changes in the designs, you will gain confidence and soon will become a great art quilter and be designing your own quilts.

NOTES TO GET YOU STARTED

The chapters are in order of difficulty. Small quilts that have Outline Designs with short, straight lines are easier to cut than large quilts having Outline Designs with long, curvy lines and big elements of design.

- Use a tightly woven fabric (such as a batik) for the Outline Design.

- Since these quilts are made as display pieces and will not need to be washed, you do not need to prewash the fabrics.

- Fabric amounts are based on 40" width.

- I use HeatnBond Lite paper-backed fusible web (17" wide).

- For quilts wider than the width of your paper-backed fusible web, use multiple widths, overlapping them ½" and taping with masking tape to create one large piece.

- Save the Outline Design cutouts to make a second quilt (see *Butterfly Garden*, page 25, and *Night Butterfly*, page 29).

- A designing board (page 89) gives a good work surface to create and design small quilts.

- When adding the small background pieces under the Outline Design, you can either pin or fuse-baste a tiny area of the pieces using a small craft iron or the tip of a regular iron (see *Diamond Cut*, Add the Fabric Background, Step 8 photo, page 23).

Outline Design Technique at a Glance

Refer to the individual projects and Basic Instructions (page 89) for more detailed instructions, information, and additional methods of technique.

1. Choose the design.

2. Trace the design onto paper-backed fusible web.

Design

Fuse the paper-backed fusible web onto the fabric that will be the Outline Design.

Background and Outline Design fabric

3. Cut out the Outline Design.

4. Remove the paper backing, position the Outline Design onto the background fabric, making sure you choose an area that gives good contrast between the Outline Design and the background. Fuse.

5. Finish the raw edges.

6. Layer with batting and backing, and quilt.

7. Bind.

Cutting Techniques
and Project Samples

CUTTING TECHNIQUES

If you take a little time to master using a craft knife to cut out the Outline Design, you will see its benefits.

Choosing a Craft Knife

I use a small, sharp craft knife created for cutting different surfaces. A few manufacturers make them: X-ACTO, Utility, and Hobby to name a few. Knives have a plastic or metal handle in different sizes and interchangeable blades in a variety of shapes and sizes. The blades are easily changeable.

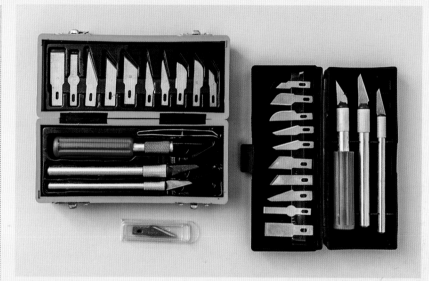

Craft knife sets

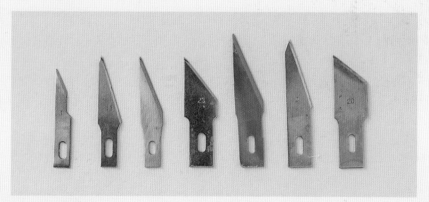

Recommended blades

Try sharp, pointed blades with different handles and choose the one you like the most. This is a personal decision; I like to use N11 in a thin handle and N23 and N2 in a big handle.

X-ACTO blades

Using a Craft Knife

When cutting, hold the craft knife between the thumb and index fingers, and rest the top of the handle between them for support.

 tip

If it feels more secure and natural, you can hold it as you would hold a pen, adding your middle finger for support when you are cutting.

Hand position for holding craft knife

 NOTE

Always start cutting ¹⁄₁₆″ or less (2–3 mm) before the cutting point and finish the cutting line ¹⁄₁₆″–¹⁄₈″ (2–3 mm) after the finish point.

1. To start cutting, point the craft knife vertically and poke it through the layers until you hear a click.

Poking position of blade

 tip

The craft knife cutting technique is similar to rotary cutting, because your shoulder, forearm, and hand work together, with only the shoulder making the gentle moves necessary to control your knife for perfect cuts. It should look and feel like a robot arm. The difference is in direction: with rotary cutting you cut from your body out. With craft knife cutting you cut from up and out—toward your body.

2. Lower the knife until your hand and the knife are parallel to the cutting board. Place your noncutting hand above the craft knife and apply medium pressure to cut through the fabric fused with paper-backed fusible web. When you are cutting, your hand will not touch the cutting surface. Reposition your noncutting hand above the craft knife every 2″ of cutting. Always check to be sure you cut through all layers.

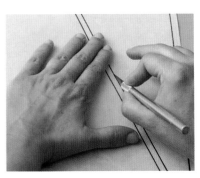

Hand position for cutting

As you get more experience you will feel more comfortable and get better results.

PROJECT SAMPLES

Let's practice cutting with a craft knife and make some great project samples while we're at it.

SAMPLE 1 *Cutting Geometric Shapes with Corner Points*

Refer to Cutting Techniques (page 9).

1. Cut 1 piece 10″ × 10″ of any color of cotton fabric (I used a black batik) and cut 1 piece 10″ × 10″ of paper-backed fusible web. Fuse them together (1 piece of fabric to the adhesive side of 1 piece of fusible web), following the manufacturer's instructions. Cut 1 piece 10″ × 10″ of colorful background fabric.

2. Using a ruler and pencil or thin marker, draw a ½″ frame around the outside edges of the fused square on the paper side (this frame will hold the pieces of the Outline Design together in one piece). Draw a variety of geometric shapes: triangles, squares, and free-form shapes with straight lines. They don't need to match the ones in the illustration below.

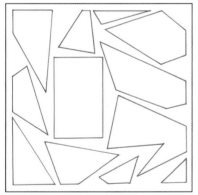

Geometric shapes

3. Attach a new N2 blade to the big craft knife (or N11 to the thin craft knife) and secure it to the handle.

4. Choose the element you want to cut first. Place the point of the knife ¹⁄₁₆″–⅛″ (2–3 mm) before the starting point of the line; poke the blade through the layers.

5. Lower the blade, hold the design with your left hand 2″ above the cutting line (see the photo under Using a Craft Knife, Step 2, page 10), and then cut to the end of the line plus ¹⁄₁₆″–⅛″ (2–3 mm). This overcutting will give you clean intersections and ensure that all the threads are cut.

Cut intersection.

 NOTE

Cut all straight lines slightly diagonally from the top left to the bottom right. Rotate your work after every cut line to be sure you always cut only vertically.

6. Cut out all of the elements, one by one, and store them in a plastic bag. Remove the paper backing. This fused-fabric piece is your Outline Design.

 NOTE

Remember to overcut the start and finish of the cutting lines ¹⁄₁₆″–⅛″ (2–3 mm).

7. Align the Outline Design on top of the background fabric and press it using an up-and-down motion with an iron set on medium heat. Do not slide the iron.

8. Using the leftover cutouts you saved in a plastic bag, choose one shape and trim ¼″ off each side using scissors. If you position it into its coordinating opening on the Outline Design, you will see that it floats in the space. You can cut and modify this piece any way you like using a craft knife or scissors (see the photo below for ideas). Continue to modify the remaining pieces in the plastic bag to make your own inside shapes. Just make sure they are smaller and allow the bright background fabric to show through.

9. Position in the Outline Design and press to fuse in place.

Sample geometric Outline Design

10. See Finishing Raw Edges of Outline Designs (page 91) to determine when to layer with batting and backing. Note: I did not bind the samples.

SAMPLE 2 *Cutting Long, Straight and Wavy Stripes*

Refer to Cutting Techniques (page 9).

1. Cut 1 piece 10″ × 10″ of any color of cotton fabric (I used a black batik) and cut 1 piece 10″ × 10″ of paper-backed fusible web. Fuse them together (1 piece of fabric to the adhesive side of 1 piece of fusible web) following the manufacturer's instructions. Cut 1 piece 10″ × 10″ of colorful background fabric.

2. Using a pencil or thin marker, draw a ½″ frame around the outside edges of the fused square on the paper side (this frame will hold the pieces of the Outline Design together in one piece). Draw wavy and straight stripes. They don't need to match the ones in the illustration below.

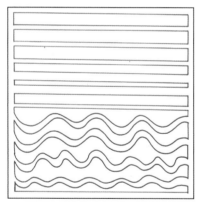

Straight and wavy stripes

3. Attach a new N2 blade to the big craft knife or N11 to the thin craft knife and secure it to the handle.

4. Choose the first shape to cut. Place the point of knife ⅟₁₆″–⅛″ (2–3 mm) before the starting point of the line; poke the blade through the layers.

5. Lower the blade, hold the design with your left hand 2″ above the cutting line (see the photo under Using a Craft Knife, Step 2, page 10), and then cut to the end of the line plus ⅟₁₆″–⅛″ (2–3 mm). This overcutting will give you clean intersections and ensure that all the threads are cut.

Cut intersection.

6. Cut out all of the elements, one by one. Remove the paper backing. This fused-fabric piece is your Outline Design.

 NOTE

Remember to overcut the start and finish of the cutting lines ⅟₁₆″ or less (2–3 mm).

7. Align the Outline Design on top of the background fabric and press it using an up-and-down motion with an iron set on medium heat. Do not slide the iron.

8. See Finishing Raw Edges of Outline Designs (page 91) to determine when to layer with batting and backing. Note: I did not bind the samples.

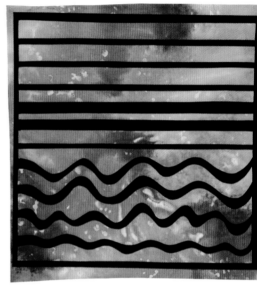

Straight and wavy stripes outline on fabric, fused to background.

Color variation

SAMPLE 3 Cutting Circles, Ovals, and Hard Curvy Shapes

Refer to Cutting Techniques (page 9).

1. Cut 1 piece 10″ × 10″ of any color of cotton fabric (I used a black batik) and cut 1 piece 10″ × 10″ of paper-backed fusible web. Fuse them together (1 piece of fabric to the adhesive side of 1 piece of fusible web) following the manufacturer's instructions. Cut 1 piece 10″ × 10″ of colorful background fabric.

2. Draw circles or semicircles with or without rulers or a compass. The stencils can be used too. See the circles and curves illustrations (at right) for ideas. I used the Easy Circle Cut ruler by Sharon Hultgren for EZ Quilting to draw the circles and curves #2 design. You don't need to match my designs.

3. Attach a new N2 blade to the big craft knife or N11 to the thin craft knife and secure it to the handle.

4. Mark the parts you will cut.

5. Choose the first shape to cut. Place the point of the knife 1/16″ or less (2–3 mm) before the starting point of the line; poke the blade through the layers. Cut only 1/4 of circle at a time and make your cuts clockwise from the top.

6. Lower the blade, hold the design with your left hand 2″ above the cutting line (see the photo under Using a Craft Knife, Step 2, page 10), and then cut to the end of the line plus 2 mm. This overcutting will give you clean intersections and ensure that all the threads are cut.

Circles and curves #1

Circles and curves #2

Cut intersection

7. Cut out all of the elements one by one and store them in a plastic bag to make the bonus project sample. Gently remove the paper backing by rolling it onto any empty paper roll (from paper towel or wrapping paper); try to keep the paper backing in one piece to use for the bonus project sample (page 15). If it tears, repair it with masking tape. The fused-fabric piece is your Outline Design.

 NOTE

Remember to overcut the start and finish of the cutting lines ¹⁄₁₆″–¹⁄₈″ (2–3 mm).

Circles and curves #1

Circles and curves #2

8. Align the Outline Design on top of the background fabric and press it using an up-and-down motion with an iron set on medium heat. Do not slide the iron.

9. See Finishing Raw Edges of Outline Designs (page 91) to determine when to layer with batting and backing. Note: I did not bind the samples.

Circles and curves #1, color variation

Bonus Project Sample

1. Unroll the paper backing from the saved Outline Design and pin it onto multicolored fabric, shiny side up.

2. Take the cutouts from the plastic bag one at a time. Remove the paper and find the exact opening for each piece. Accurately fill it in with fabric, right side up, like a puzzle. When you fill up all openings, press with an iron set on medium heat; then remove the paper.

You have the negative work of art, made from the cutout shapes. If you decide to make a big quilt using this technique, you can make the second quilt from the cutout shapes, or modify the inserted shapes, like in the Sample geometric Outline Design (page 11).

Circles and curves #2, negative variation

Negative variation

Process Overview

POPPY BLOOM

CHAPTER 2

FINISHED QUILT: 16″ × 16″

This is a small project to try the Outline Design technique. It is a simple but colorful way to learn how to use new tools, to practice, and to make you confident.

Before starting your project, read Introduction (page 6) and Basic Instructions (page 89).

MATERIALS

- Black fabric (I used black batik): 18″ × 18″ or a fat quarter

- Rainbow gradation fabric: ½ yard *or* Colorful fat quarters: red, orange, yellow, green, blue, and purple, and 2″ × 2″ green polka dot

- Paper-backed fusible web (such as HeatnBond Lite): 2 pieces 17″ × 17″

- Batting: 18″ × 18″ of low loft

- Backing: 18″ × 18″

- Binding: ¼ yard

- Clear cellophane wrapping paper: 1 yard

- Very thin, navy blue tulle (optional): 18″ × 18″

Gradation fabric

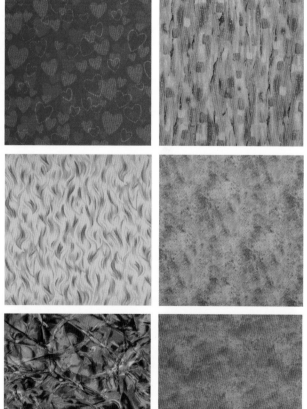

6 colorful fat quarters

2″ × 2″ green polka dot

CREATE THE OUTLINE DESIGN PATTERN

1. On the paper side of the fusible web, draw with a pencil (or fold) straight lines vertically and horizontally to divide the square into quarters. Draw wavy vertical and horizontal lines over the straight lines. Draw wavy diagonal lines from corner to corner through the center point. Now you have 8 wedges.

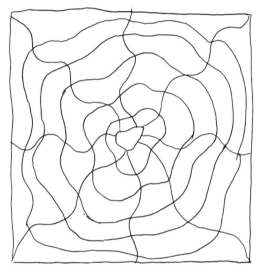

Poppy Bloom drawing

2. Draw a ½" frame around the square with a ¼"-wide marker. Draw a small 1½" circular shape in the center. Do not try to make it perfect. Now, draw the 8 curvy lines from your circle to the sides over the center lines and to the corners of the square.

Poppy Bloom Outline Design pattern

3. Draw the 5 curvy circular shapes (you can do it with pencil first, if you prefer).

CUT OUT THE OUTLINE DESIGN

1. Center the Outline Design on the wrong side of the black fabric. Fuse it by ironing on both the paper and fabric sides, following the manufacturer's directions. Check to make sure it fused across the entire piece. Let it cool.

2. Refer to Cutting Techniques (page 9) to cut out the design. Place the cutouts into a plastic bag; you can use them for a second project (see *Butterfly Garden*, page 25, and *Night Butterfly*, page 29).

3. Do not remove the paper backing yet. Mark the top, bottom, left, and right.

Fuse Outline Design onto black fabric.

ADD THE FABRIC BACKGROUND

1. Place the Outline Design, fabric side up, onto the fusible side of the second piece of fusible web.

Place cut Outline Design (fabric side up) onto second piece of fusible web (fusible side up).

2. Lay the clear cellophane over the design.

Lay cellophane over design.

METHOD 1 *Using a Gradation Fabric*

1. Trace each of the 8 wedges onto the cellophane paper separately, one at a time, ⅛" bigger around than the shape you see (in the windows), using a black fine-point permanent marker. The marker line will be in the middle of the design lines.

2. Cut the wedges from the cellophane on the drawn line, one at a time. Write the letter R on each piece, place it on the right side of the colorful fabric, and pin. The point of every wedge should be on the same line of color.

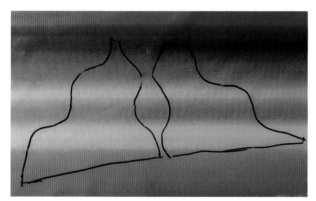

Wedges on gradation fabric

3. Cut out one wedge with scissors, cutting exactly on the marked line.

4. Place it in position, under the black fabric Outline Design and on top of the fusible web, using tweezers, if necessary. Pin it to the fusible web.

5. Repeat Steps 3 and 4 for each wedge, one at a time, so you know where each one belongs.

Place wedges one by one under Outline Design on top of fusible web, pin to the web, or heat point with small iron.

6. Carefully lift only the Outline Design and remove the paper backing. Put it back over the color fabrics. Check to be sure all the pieces are aligned. Use tweezers to move the shapes under the Outline Design.

7. Set the iron on the Cotton or Wool setting and press using an up-and-down motion consistently over the whole quilt top. Turn it over and press the paper backing too. Let it cool. Remove the paper from the back.

8. Center the quilt top on top of the batting and fuse.

Quilting detail

....

METHOD 2 *Using Fat Quarters*

1. Trace the whole curvy circles for each color onto cellophane, one at a time, ⅛″ bigger around than the shape you see (in the windows). The marker line will be in the middle of the design lines. Mark the top and bottom.

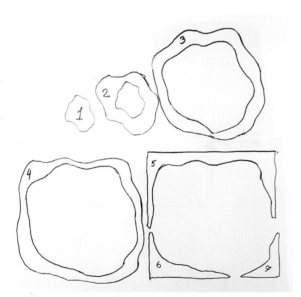

Trace curvy circles onto cellophane.

2. Pin each circle onto the right side of the fabric. Cut on the drawn lines.

3. Remove the paper backing from the Outline Design. Position the fabric circles under the Outline Design. Press the layers together on both the fabric and the paper side. Remove the paper backing.

4. Place the fused quilt top onto the batting and press them together.

Multiple fabric variation

FINISHING

1. See Finishing Raw Edges of Outline Designs (page 91). I used Method 3: Tulle-Covered Design (page 92).

2. Layer, quilt, square up the quilt, and bind.

Level-One Quilt Projects

DIAMOND CUT

FINISHED QUILT: 22″ × 22″

Diamond Cut *is a geometric design with straight, easy-to-cut lines. The Outline Design is symmetrical four ways. The repeated elements make it easy to cut by combining them together a few at a time. The background pieces were cut out one by one and positioned between the Outline Design and the batting, like painting by number. The color variations are endless; I hope you will enjoy experimenting with colors.*

Before starting your project, read Introduction (page 6) and Basic Instructions (page 89). For more detailed instructions, refer to Chapter 2: Process Overview—Poppy Bloom (page 16).

MATERIALS

- Black fabric (I used black batik): 22″ × 22″

- Gradation colored fabrics (1 or more): 1 yard total or fat quarters in variety of colors

- Paper-backed fusible web (such as Heat*n*Bond Lite): 2⅝ yards

- Batting: 24″ × 24″ of low loft

- Backing: 24″ × 24″

- Binding: ¼ yard

- Clear cellophane wrapping paper: 1 yard

- Very thin, navy blue tulle (optional): 22″ × 22″

Gradation-colored fabrics

CREATE THE OUTLINE DESIGN PATTERN

1. Create 1 sheet of the fusible web 22″ × 22″ by connecting 2 pieces with masking tape. Repeat to make a second sheet 24″ × 24″.

2. Trace the *Diamond Cut* Outline Design pattern (page 24) onto the paper side of fusible web.

CUT OUT THE OUTLINE DESIGN

1. Center the Outline Design pattern on the wrong side of the black fabric. Fuse it by ironing on both the paper and fabric sides, following the manufacturer's directions. Check to make sure it fused across the entire piece. Let it cool.

2. Refer to Cutting Techniques (page 9) to cut out the design.

3. Do not remove the paper backing yet.

ADD THE FABRIC BACKGROUND

1. Attach the backing fabric onto the batting with mounting adhesive.

2. Fuse the second piece of fusible web onto the batting, following the manufacturer's instructions. Let it cool. Remove the paper backing from the batting.

3. Align the Outline Design on top of the fused side of the batting (fabric side up) and pin in the corners.

4. Place the cellophane paper over the largest element. Usually, when I use the gradations, I combine a few elements together and insert larger pieces first, then add the small ones under the Outline Design, on top of the larger shape.

5. Trace each shape onto the cellophane paper separately, one at a time, 1/8" bigger around than the shape you see (in the windows), using a black fine-point permanent marker. The marker line will be in the middle of the design lines. If any elements are repeated in the design, write on the cellophane pattern the number of pieces you need to cut.

6. Place this pattern onto the fabric and pin. Cut with scissors.

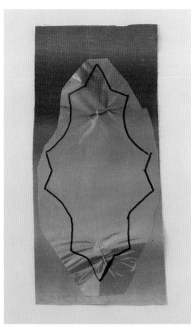

Pin pattern to right side of fabric and cut on marked line.

 tip

If you need to cut several pieces of the same shape and fabric, fold the fabric so that you have 4 layers and pin. If you need 8 of the same elements, cut 4 at a time. If the elements are mirror images, cut half of them, flip the cellophane pattern over, and cut the other half.

7. Insert the elements one by one. Use tweezers to gently slide them under the Outline Design.

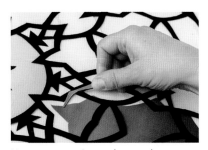

Use tweezers to insert elements between batting and Outline Design.

8. Iron-baste each piece using a small crafter's iron or the tip of an iron on 2 points as you insert them. Try not to touch the Outline Design dividing strips with a hot iron at this stage or they will stick before you're ready. If you need to correct the placement of some of the pieces, just pull them up and position them correctly.

Baste to fusible with small iron in 2 places.

9. Add the small elements on top of the larger elements and under the Outline Design.

10. Remove the paper backing from the Outline Design and put it back over the background collage fabrics. Check alignment.

11. Set the iron on the Cotton or Wool setting and press using an up-and-down motion consistently over the whole quilt top. Let it cool.

FINISHING

1. See Finishing Raw Edges of Outline Designs (page 91). I used Method 3: Tulle-Covered Design (page 92).

2. Layer, quilt, square up the quilt, and bind.

Diamond Cut Outline Design pattern (enlarge 300%)

BUTTERFLY GARDEN

FINISHED QUILT: 20″ × 20″

Butterfly Garden is an example of an organic design. The technique I used is slightly different from the other projects in this book. I added the theatrical fabrics in only some of the sections—leaves, flowers, and wings on top of a wholecloth, multicolored print background—rather than filling in all of the sections individually on top of the batting. This gives more dimensionality to the quilt by making the background recede. This quilt also gives you the perfect opportunity to save the cutouts to make a second quilt (see Night Butterfly, page 29).

Before starting your project, read Introduction (page 6) and Basic Instructions (page 89). For more detailed instructions, refer to Chapter 2: Process Overview—Poppy Bloom (page 16).

MATERIALS

- Black fabric (I used black batik): 20″ × 20″
- Colorful fabric: 22″ × 22″
- Green-blue gradation: 1 fat quarter
- Pink-yellow gradation: 1 fat quarter
- Black fabric with polka dots: 2″ × 10″

- Theatrical fabric: for embellishment on various colors, 10″ × 10″ of each color: teal, gold tone, green, yellow green, and turquoise light blue
- Backing: 22″ × 22″
- Batting, low loft: 22″ × 22″

- Binding: ¼ yard
- Paper-backed fusible web (such as Heat*n*Bond Lite): 2 yards × 17″
- Clear cellophane wrapping paper: 1 yard

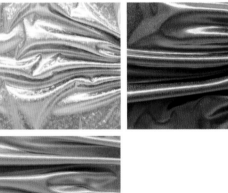

Theatrical fabrics

Fabrics

CREATE THE OUTLINE DESIGN PATTERN

1. Create 1 sheet of the fusible web 20″ × 20″ by connecting 2 pieces with masking tape.

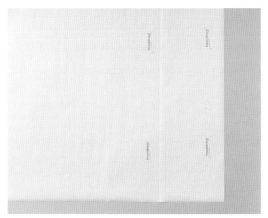

Tape 2 pieces of fusible web with masking tape on paper side to make 1 larger sheet.

2. Trace the *Butterfly Garden* Outline Design pattern (pullout page P1) onto the paper side of the fusible web.

3. Center the Outline Design pattern on the wrong side of the black fabric. Fuse it by ironing on both the paper and fabric sides, following the manufacturer's directions. Check to make sure it fused across the entire piece. Let it cool.

CUT OUT THE OUTLINE DESIGN

1. Refer to Cutting Techniques (page 9) to cut out the design. Place the cutouts into a plastic bag to make *Night Butterfly* (page 29).

2. Remove the paper backing.

 NOTE

If you want to make Night Butterfly *(page 29), carefully remove the paper backing, little by little, by rolling it onto an empty paper roll, or any roll from wrapping paper. Save the paper backing pattern. If the paper rips, fix it with masking tape.*

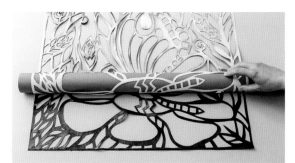

Remove paper using a paper roll.

ADD THE FABRIC BACKGROUND

1. Layer the background fabric, batting, and backing using basting spray (see Basting the Quilt Layers, page 90).

2. Align the Outline Design on top of the background fabric and pin it in the 4 corners.

Outline Design on background fabric

ADD THE EXTRA WING LAYERS

1. Place the cellophane paper over the butterfly wings on your quilt top. Using a black fine-line permanent marker, draw the shape of one wing ⅛″ bigger around than the shape you see (in the windows). The marker line will be in the middle of the design lines.

Draw wing shape on cellophane paper.

2. Cut this shape from the cellophane on the marked line.

3. Iron fusible web to the wrong side of the green-blue gradation and pink-yellow gradation fat quarters.

4. Place the cellophane pattern onto the right side of the green-blue fused fabric. Pin together and cut out with scissors.

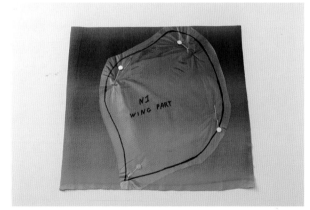

Draw wing shape on cellophane paper.

5. Position the cut shape under the Outline Design, using tweezers, if necessary.

6. Follow the same process to create the other 2 parts of the wings and the flower petals.

7. Iron fusible web to the wrong side of the theatrical fabrics. Remember, they are heat sensitive.

8. Following the same process, create the leaves, gold-tone spots on the wings, body, and second flower.

9. Slide the cut elements under the Outline Design through the largest openings; always use tweezers. Gently move the small pieces under the Outline Design until everything looks perfect.

10. Iron-baste each piece, using a small craft iron or the tip of an iron, on 2 points as you insert it. (Use the Teflon sheet or piece of pressing cloth for theatrical fabrics.) Try not to touch the Outline Design dividing strips with the iron at this stage or they will stick before you're ready. If you need to correct the placement of some of the pieces, just pull them up and position them correctly.

11. Check to be sure all the pieces are aligned. Use tweezers to move the shapes under the Outline Design.

12. Set the iron on the Cotton or Wool setting and press using an up-and-down motion consistently over the whole quilt top. Let it cool. Because the theatrical fabrics are heat sensitive, they must be pressed using a Teflon, fabric, or paper pressing sheet.

FINISHING

1. See Finishing Raw Edges of Outline Designs (page 91). I used Method 1: Couched Raw Edges (page 91).

2. Layer, quilt, square up the quilt, and bind.

NIGHT BUTTERFLY

FINISHED QUILT: 20″ × 20″

*I created **Night Butterfly** as an experiment to use the cutouts from one quilt (Butterfly Garden, page 25) to make a second one. I placed the leftover pattern backing paper from Butterfly Garden on top of the same colorful background fabric (shiny side up) as in Butterfly Garden and added the black cutouts (paper removed) in the coordinating position. It was fun to find the appropriate places for every cutout element. I trimmed away the centers of the larger pieces, so more of the background fabric could show through. This quilt cleverly uses the cutouts from Butterfly Garden.*

Before starting your project, read Introduction (page 6) and Basic Instructions (page 89). For more detailed instructions, refer to Chapter 2: Process Overview—Poppy Bloom (page 16).

MATERIALS

- Multicolored bright fabric: 20″ × 20″ for Outline Design
- Backing: 22″ × 22″
- Batting: 22″ × 22″ low loft

- Binding: ¼ yard
- Removed paper from Outline Design of *Butterfly Garden* (page 25)

- All cutout elements from Outline Design from *Butterfly Garden*
- Very thin, navy blue tulle (optional): 22″ × 22″

Fabric for background

Detail of *Night Butterfly*

LAYER THE QUILT

1. Make the quilt sandwich from background fabric, batting, and backing.

2. Place the paper pattern onto the quilt sandwich, shiny side up. Pin in the corners.

3. Take the curved elements one by one, remove the paper backing, and place them into position.

4. Iron-baste each piece, using a small craft iron or the tip of an iron, on 2 points as you insert it. Try not to touch the Outline Design dividing strips with the iron at this stage or they will stick before you're ready. If you need to correct the placement of some of the pieces, just pull them up and position them correctly.

5. Set the iron on the Cotton or Wool setting and press using an up-and-down motion consistently over the whole quilt top. Let it cool.

FINISHING

1. See Finishing Raw Edges of Outline Designs (page 91). I used Method 3: Tulle-Covered Design (page 92).

2. Layer, quilt, square up the quilt, and bind.

Pattern placed on top of quilt sandwich

 NOTE

If you want a more colorful look, you can cut off most of the center of the big flower petals (using scissors) to remove most of the black fabric.

Center can be cut from flower petals.

On one of my visits to the Bronx Zoo, I took photographs of the butterflies. As I was transferring my pictures to my computer, I was inspired to create a quilt design with elements of butterfly wings.

I sketched many details of the butterfly wings. Then, I repeated vertical and horizontal mirror images to create a simple, graphic sketch using curvy lines to combine the complimentary geometric shapes. This became the Outline Design pattern for the quilt.

I created the Outline Design using black fabric and added very bright fabric in a variety of complementary color gradations to fill in the sections. Since this quilt is bigger than the fabric width, I made the wings, triangles, and center from separate pieces of fabric. The raw edges are finished with couching over metallic yarn with transparent thread (see Method 1: Couched Raw Edges, page 91). I quilted the inserted elements with microstippling using silk threads in matching colors.

Inspiration **PRIMROSE** FINISHED QUILT: 50″ × 50½″

Primrose was inspired by a visit to Notre-Dame de Paris. The stained-glass window in the cathedral looked beautiful; the sun came through it and embellished everything around it. I translated the stained glass to make a circular design.

I used complementary colors in a variety of values of gradated fabrics in greens and reds, light on dark, and dark on light for exciting contrast.

I couched black yarn over the raw edges with clear transparent thread (see Method 1: Couch the Raw Edges, page 91) and finished it with free-motion quilting.

Gradation fabric, detail

I made a photo of *Funky Reef* (page 80) and processed it using Kaleidoscope Kreator 3 (kalcollections.com), a special program for quilters to help create kaleidoscopic designs. I used a lucky wedge, ⅟₁₆ of the circle from *Funky Reef,* and then mirror-imaged, paired, and repeated it 8 times around the center to create the Outline Design pattern for *Tulip Fields*. I saved it as a large file so I could easily enlarge the pattern.

Lucky wedge on *Funky Reef*

Next, I processed the image through Adobe Photoshop to make it a rectangular shape. I chose one of the "Skinny" options to create the Outline Design pattern.

I printed it out in black-and-white (lowering the brightness to save on ink) as a poster, using multiple 8½″ × 11″ Quilter's Freezer Paper Sheets (by C&T Publishing) to create the 64″ × 42″ Outline Design pattern. I followed the basic technique to make the quilt, except I ironed fusible web to each colored fabric shape rather than adding fusible web to the batting.

I finished the raw edges with couching over metallic yarn with transparent thread (see Method 1: Couch the Raw Edges, page 91). I quilted it with microstippling using silk threads in matching colors.

Tulip Fields quilting detail

Inspiration for this quilt came from a group of jewelry workshops in Rio de Janeiro, where masters cut and shape beautiful green, yellow, red, and blue precious stones. I like to see the rainbow effect created when the sunlight comes through the stones. It took a long time to find the right silky, sateen fabric printed with a gradation of these bright colors, but I found it in Russia. I bought 5 yards because I knew I would never find the same fabric again.

The design includes geometric elements related to diamonds or a princess cut of precious stones. I combined geometric figures, straight lines, circles, and ovals into a square composition in the frame. I drew ⅛ of the design and made a kaleidoscope as a circle in the square using Kaleidoscope Kreator 3 (kalcollections.com) and Adobe Photoshop to stretch the design into a rect-angle, creating an oval center. I printed the Outline Design pattern in multiple pages as a poster and traced the design on quilt-size fusible web. For more construction guidance, see the project instructions for *Rosy Bloom* (page 62).

I finished the raw edges by couching gold-tan metallic yarn with clear thread and added Swarovski crystals.

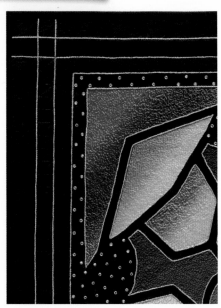

Detail of *Emerald City*

Level-Two Quilt Projects

CITY SCAPE

FINISHED QUILT: 21½″ × 21½″

This project is simple to make. Personalize the details or skip some of the window-frame details. You can add the streetlights, people, trees, or signs.

Before starting your project, read Introduction (page 6) and Basic Instructions (page 89). For more detailed instructions, refer to Chapter 2: Process Overview—Poppy Bloom (page 16).

MATERIALS

- Black fabric: 22″ × 22″
- Black-gray gradation: fat quarter or light, medium, and darker shades of the same color, like gray, brown, dark purple and so on
- Multicolored print: 1 fat quarter for windows
- Orange gradation: 1 fat quarter for the sky
- Paper-backed fusible web (such as Heat*n*Bond Lite): 2⅝ yards × 17″
- Backing: 24″ × 24″
- Batting: 24″ × 24″ of low loft
- Binding: ¼ yard
- Clear cellophane wrapping paper: 1 yard
- Very thin, navy blue tulle (optional): 24″ × 24″

CREATE THE OUTLINE DESIGN PATTERN

1. Create 1 sheet of the fusible web 22″ × 22″ by connecting 2 pieces with masking tape. Repeat to make a second sheet 24″ × 24″.

2. Trace the *City Scape* Outline Design pattern (page 41) onto the paper side of fusible web.

3. Fuse the Outline Design onto the black fabric following the manufacturer's instructions.

CUT OUT THE OUTLINE DESIGN

1. Center the Outline Design on the wrong side of the black fabric. Fuse it by ironing on both the paper and fabric sides, following the manufacturer's directions. Check to make sure it fused across the entire piece. Let it cool.

2. Refer to Cutting Techniques (page 9) to cut out the design.

3. Remove the paper backing.

Use a nonslip ruler and the craft knife or a rotary cutter to help you cut straight lines.

ADD THE FABRIC BACKGROUND

1. Fuse the other piece of fusible web onto the batting, let it cool, and remove the paper backing.

2. Position the Outline Design right side up on the fused side of the batting and pin in the 4 corners.

3. Place the cellophane paper over the sky section on your quilt top. Using a black fine-line permanent marker, draw the sky shape ⅛" bigger around than the shape you see (in the windows). The marker line will be in the middle of the design lines.

4. Cut this shape from the cellophane on the marked line.

5. Place the cellophane pattern onto the right side of the sky fabric. Pin them together and cut it out on the line with scissors.

6. Using tweezers, slide the sky fabric between the Outline Design and fused batting.

7. All of the building's windows are one piece of multicolored fabric. Trace the shape of the combined group of buildings as one big shape onto cellophane (see Step 3) and pin it to the window fabric.

8. Cut it out on the line with scissors.

9. Position it under the Outline Design and pin.

10. Trace and cut out the street piece(s), referring to Steps 3–7, using the street fabric.

 NOTE

You can embellish the windows by adding shiny metallic, luminescent, or decorative pieces.

11. Set the iron on the Cotton or Wool setting and press using an up-and-down motion consistently over the whole quilt top. Let it cool.

FINISHING

1. See Finishing Raw Edges of Outline Designs (page 91). I used Method 3: Tulle-Covered Design (page 92) and quilted on the Outline Design dividing lines and in the open spaces such as the sky and street.

2. Layer, quilt, square up the quilt, and bind.

 NOTE

I would not recommend finishing with couching, but you can leave the edges raw and add microstippling, which would certainly look great.

City Scape detail

City Scape color variation

City Scape Outline Design pattern (enlarge 300%)

FARM LAND

FINISHED QUILT: 21″ × 21¾″

The project looks very simple, but the color combination, number of the fabrics for spaces to fill, and dividing lines, which are very thin, will make this project more of a challenge. If you want to make the dividing lines wider, just draw them wider when you trace the Outline Design pattern onto the paper-backed fusible web. I used 25 pieces of fabric in different colors and prints. Feel free to personalize this design by adding elements to reflect your own life.

Before starting your project, read Introduction (page 6) and Basic Instructions (page 89). For more detailed instructions, refer to Chapter 2: Process Overview—Poppy Bloom (page 16).

MATERIALS

- **Black fabric:** 21″ × 22″

- **Green fabric:** Scraps of 15 different shades and tints

- **Blue-purple fabric:** 4 scraps in various sizes to fit individual pieces

- **Yellow-orange fabric:** 5 scraps in various sizes to fit individual pieces

- **Paper-backed fusible web** (such as Heat*n*Bond Lite): 2½ yards × 17″

- **Backing:** 23″ × 24″

- **Batting:** 23″ × 24″ of low loft

- **Binding:** ¼ yard

- **Clear cellophane wrapping paper:** 2 yards

- **Very thin, navy blue tulle (optional):** 23″ × 24″

CREATE THE OUTLINE DESIGN PATTERN

1. Create 1 sheet of the fusible web 21″ × 22″ by connecting 2 pieces with masking tape. Repeat to make a second sheet 23″ × 24″.

2. Trace the *Farm Land* Outline Design pattern (page 45) onto the paper side of fusible web.

3. Fuse the Outline Design onto the black fabric following the manufacturer's instructions.

CUT OUT THE OUTLINE DESIGN

1. Center the Outline Design on the wrong side of the black fabric. Fuse it by ironing on both the paper and fabric sides, following the manufacturer's directions. Check to make sure it fused across the entire piece. Let it cool.

2. Refer to Cutting Techniques (page 9) to cut out the design.

3. Remove the paper backing.

ADD THE FABRIC BACKGROUND

1. Fuse the other piece of fusible web onto the batting, let it cool, and remove the paper backing.

2. Position the Outline Design on the fused side of the batting and pin in the 4 corners.

3. Choose the sections of the design you want to include on each fabric. Trace each section onto the cellophane paper separately, one at a time, ⅛" bigger around than the shape you see (in the landscape), using a black fine-point permanent marker. The marker line will be in the middle of the design lines.

4. Cut the pieces from the cellophane a little bigger than the drawn line, one at a time. Write the letter R on the cellophane. Place it on the right side of the colorful fabric and pin.

5. Cut out the shapes on the drawn line and insert them between the Outline Design and the batting using tweezers, if necessary, and pin.

6. Place the cellophane patterns onto the right side of the fabrics. Pin and cut out on the lines with scissors.

7. Using tweezers, slide the sky fabric between the Outline Design and fused batting.

8. Iron-baste each piece, using a small craft iron or the tip of an iron, on 2 points as you insert it. Try not to touch the Outline Design dividing strips with the iron at this stage or they will stick before you're ready. If you need to correct the placement of some of the pieces, just pull them up and position them correctly.

9. Check to be sure all the pieces are aligned. Use tweezers to move the shapes under the Outline Design.

10. Set the iron on the Cotton or Wool setting and press using an up-and-down motion consistently over the whole quilt top. Let it cool.

FINISHING

1. See Finishing Raw Edges of Outline Designs (page 91). I used Method 3: Tulle-Covered Design (page 92).

2. Layer, quilt, square up the quilt, and bind.

Farm Land color variation

Farm Land Outline Design pattern (enlarge 300%)

STILL LIFE

FINISHED QUILT: 21″ × 21″

I always think about the composition of a design first; this one is made as a triangle. I drew the curtains and a section of the table to show perspective. A simple vase, and flowers you cannot identify, make this design attractive because the flowers are bigger than in real life and the colors I chose are complementary to contrast in value. If you want to personalize this quilt, refer to Designing Your Own Outline-Design Quilt (page 82).

Before starting your project, read Introduction (page 6) and Basic Instructions (page 89). For more detailed instructions, refer to Chapter 2: Process Overview—Poppy Bloom (page 16).

MATERIALS

- **Black fabric (I used a batik):** 21″ × 21″
- **Blue-green print:** ¼ yard for the view from window
- **Light print:** ½ yard for curtain (use right and wrong side for the value change)
- **Light batik:** ¼″ for the table cover
- **Bright prints:** scraps for the flowers and fruits
- **Dark gradation:** ¼ yard for the vase and teacup
- **Paper-backed fusible web (such as Heat***n***Bond Lite):** 2½ yards
- **Batting:** 23″ × 23″
- **Backing:** 23″ × 23″
- **Binding:** ¼ yard
- **Clear cellophane wrapping paper:** 2 yards

CREATE THE OUTLINE DESIGN PATTERN

1. Create 1 sheet of the fusible web 21″ × 21″ by connecting 2 pieces with masking tape. Repeat to make a second sheet 23″ × 23″.

2. Trace the *Still Life* Outline Design pattern (page 49) onto the paper side of fusible web.

3. Fuse the Outline Design onto the black fabric, following the manufacturer's instructions.

PREPARE THE CELLOPHANE PATTERNS

1. Trace the shapes of the view from the window as one big shape. Trace the curtain shapes and the table shape onto cellophane separately, one at a time, ⅛″ bigger around than the shape you see (in the windows), using a black fine-point permanent marker. The marker line will be in the middle of the design lines.

2. Pin the patterns onto the appropriate fabrics and cut them out. Set them aside.

CUT OUT THE OUTLINE DESIGN

1. Center the Outline Design on the wrong side of the black fabric. Fuse it by ironing on both the paper and fabric sides, following the manufacturer's directions. Check to make sure it fused across the entire piece. Let it cool.

2. Refer to Cutting Techniques (page 9) to cut out the design.

3. Do not remove the paper backing yet.

ADD THE FABRIC BACKGROUND

1. Fuse the other piece of fusible web onto the batting, let it cool, and remove the paper backing.

2. Cover the batting, fused side up, with the window background, curtain, and table cover fabrics. *Do not iron!*

3. Remove the paper backing from the Outline Design, position it on top of the batting, and pin in the 4 corners.

4. Trace the fruits, flowers, leaves, vase, and teacup shapes separately onto cellophane, one at a time, ⅛″ bigger around than the shape you see (in the windows), using a black fine-point permanent marker. The marker line will be in the middle of the design lines. Write the letter R on every transferred element. (This is so you will not be confused with the mirror-image pieces when you cut the fabrics.)

5. Pin the pattern onto the appropriate previously fused fabrics (chosen for all the objects on the table), cut on the marked line, and slide the shapes between the Outline Design and the background. Put 2 pins on each shape vertically.

6. Check to be sure all the pieces are aligned. Use tweezers to move the shapes under the Outline Design.

7. Set the iron on the Cotton or Wool setting and press using an up-and-down motion consistently over the whole quilt top. Let it cool.

FINISHING

1. See Finishing Raw Edges of Outline Designs (page 91). I used Method 1: Couched Raw Edges (page 91) with black metallic yarn.

2. Layer, quilt, square up the quilt, and bind.

Still Life color variation

Still Life Outline Design pattern (enlarge 300%)

BLUE RAIN

FINISHED QUILT: 25¼" × 19"

Have fun deciding what colorful fabrics you will use to fill the windows and the building elements. You can use one fabric for each building or smaller pieces of a larger variety of fabrics to fill smaller areas. To embellish the quilt, you can use the metallic, theatrical holographic fabric to make some areas glow. In the Blue Rain color variation (page 52), I painted light reflections on the foreground with fabric paints.

Before starting your project, read Introduction (page 6) and Basic Instructions (page 89). For more detailed instructions, refer to Chapter 2: Process Overview—Poppy Bloom (page 16).

MATERIALS

- Black fabric (I used a batik): 26" × 19"
- Blue fabric: 25" × 12" for sky
- Blue-purple fabric: 25" × 10" for ground

- Variety of bright colors: scraps for buildings
- Luminescent fabric: scraps for streetlights
- Paper-backed fusible web (such as Heat*n*Bond Lite): 2¼ yards

- Batting: 27" × 21" of low loft
- Backing: 27" × 21"
- Binding: ¼ yard
- Clear cellophane wrapping paper: 1½ yards

CREATE THE OUTLINE DESIGN PATTERN

1. Create 1 sheet of the fusible web 26" × 19" by connecting 2 pieces with masking tape. Repeat to make a second sheet 27" × 21".

2. Trace the *Blue Rain* Outline Design pattern (page 53) onto the paper backing side of the fusible web.

3. Fuse the Outline Design onto the black fabric, following the manufacturer's instructions.

CUT OUT THE OUTLINE DESIGN

1. Center the Outline Design on the wrong side of the black fabric. Fuse it by ironing on both the paper and fabric sides, following the manufacturer's directions. Check to make sure it fused across the entire piece. Let it cool.

2. Refer to Cutting Techniques (page 9) to cut out the design. However, a craft knife rather than scissors is necessary for this project.

3. Remove the paper backing.

ADD THE FABRIC BACKGROUND

1. Fuse the other piece of fusible web onto the batting, let it cool, and remove the paper backing. You can use this paper when fusing the entire quilt top.

2. Position the Outline Design on the fused side of the batting and pin in the 4 corners.

3. Choose the sections of the design you want to include on each fabric; it can be a few windows or an entire building. Trace each section onto the cellophane paper separately, one at a time, ⅛" bigger around than the shape you see (in the windows), using a black fine-point permanent marker. The marker line will be in the middle of the design lines.

4. Cut the pieces from the cellophane on the drawn line, one at the time, a little bigger than marked. Write the letter R on each cellophane piece. Place it on the right side of the colorful fabric and pin.

5. Cut out the shapes and insert them between the Outline Design and the batting, using tweezers, if necessary, and pin.

6. Repeat Steps 3–5 for the sky and ground shapes.

7. Check to be sure that all the pieces are aligned. Use tweezers to move the shapes under the Outline Design.

8. Set the iron on the Cotton or Wool setting and press using an up-and-down motion consistently over the whole quilt top. Let it cool.

9. Add fabric paint or prefused fabric snippets to show the light reflection on the wet foreground.

FINISHING

1. See Finishing Raw Edges of Outline Designs (page 91; see Note about quilting over raw edges).

2. Layer. I left the raw edges and quilted vertical (diagonal optional) lines to show rain, using clear thread. Square up the quilt and bind.

Blue Rain color variation

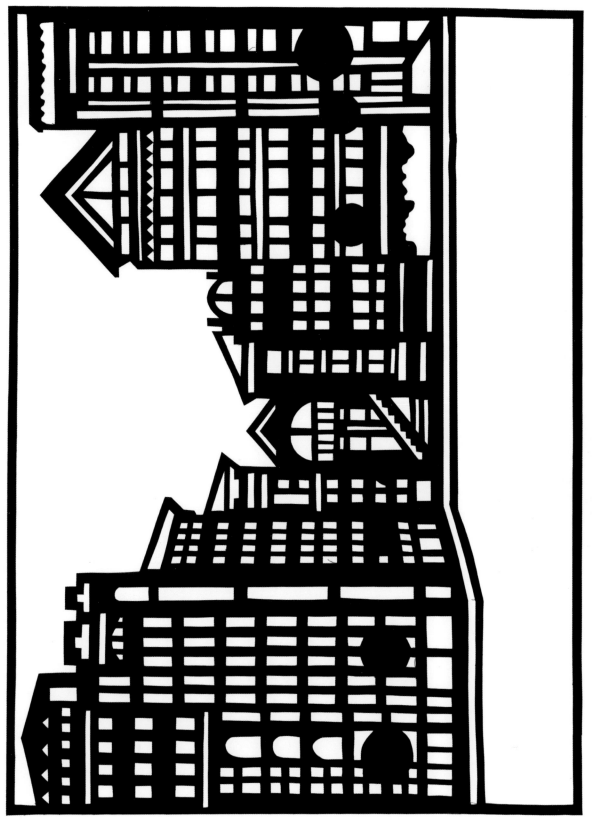

Blue Rain Outline Design pattern (enlarge 300%)

INDIAN SUMMER

FINISHED QUILT: 20˝ × 20˝

The design for Indian Summer *was inspired by a traditional feather quilting design. The brightly colored fabrics remind me of summer.*

Before starting your project, read Introduction (page 6) and Basic Instructions (page 89). For more detailed instructions, refer to Chapter 2: Process Overview—Poppy Bloom (page 16).

MATERIALS

- Black fabric (I used a batik): 20˝ × 20˝
- **Bright colors:** scraps
- **Multicolored fabric print with small objects:** 1 fat quarter
- **Paper-backed fusible web (such as Heat***n***Bond Lite):** 2⅓ yards
- **Batting:** 22˝ × 22˝ of low loft
- **Backing:** 22˝ × 22˝
- **Binding:** ¼ yard
- **Clear cellophane wrapping paper:** 1 yard

CREATE THE OUTLINE DESIGN PATTERN

1. Create 1 sheet of the fusible web 20˝ × 20˝ by connecting 2 pieces with masking tape. Repeat to make a second sheet 22˝ × 22˝.

2. Trace the *Indian Summer* Outline Design pattern (pullout page P2) onto the paper side of fusible web.

3. Fuse the Outline Design onto the black fabric, following the manufacturer's instructions.

CUT OUT THE OUTLINE DESIGN

1. Center the Outline Design on the wrong side of the black fabric. Fuse it by ironing on both the paper and fabric sides, following the manufacturer's directions. Check to make sure it fused across the entire piece. Let it cool.

2. Refer to Cutting Techniques (page 9) to cut out the design.

3. Remove the paper backing.

ADD THE FABRIC BACKGROUND

1. Fuse the other piece of fusible web onto the batting, let it cool, and remove the paper backing.

2. Position the Outline Design over the fused side of batting and pin in the 4 corners.

3. Choose the sections of the design you want to include on each fabric; it can be small or larger areas. Trace each section onto the cellophane paper separately, one at a time, ⅛" bigger around than the shape you see (in the windows), using a black fine-point permanent marker. The marker line will be in the middle of the design lines.

4. Cut the pieces from the cellophane bigger than the drawn line, one at a time. Write the letter R on each cellophane piece. Place it on the right side of the colorful fabric and pin.

5. Cut out the shapes and insert them between the Outline Design and the batting, using tweezers, if necessary, and pin. Add the small multicolored elements.

6. Carefully lift the outline design only and remove the paper backing. Put it back over the colored fabrics. Check to be sure all the pieces are aligned. Use tweezers to move the shapes under the Outline Design.

7. Set the iron on the Cotton or Wool setting and press using an up-and-down motion consistently over the whole quilt top. Let it cool.

You can use gradation fabrics for larger sections of each quarter of the design. You will need to make 4 pieces cut in the right orientation, 4 pieces cut in the mirror image, and 4 pieces for the corners. You can cut 4 at a time; just put all layers of fabric right side up.

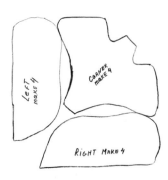

Combined left, right, and center elements on cellophane

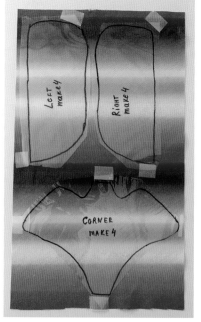

Pattern placement on fabric

Color variation with gradations (shown in ¼ of design)

FINISHING

1. See Finishing Raw Edges of Outline Designs (page 91).
I used Method 1: Couched Raw Edges (page 91).

2. Layer, quilt, square up the quilt, and bind.

Color variation (shown in ¼ of design)

LAZY-CRAZY

FINISHED QUILT: 20¾" × 21¼"

This project looks like a traditional crazy quilt, but my technique is completely different from the traditional way of making a crazy quilt. The process to make this quilt is also different from the process for the other projects in this book and includes making a collage of fabrics and then creating the Outline Design for the collaged pieces, which is my preference. Another option is to make the Outline Design pattern first and then fill the curved openings with fabrics, which more closely follows the process for the other quilts in this book.

Before starting your project, read Introduction (page 6) and Basic Instructions (page 89). For more detailed instructions, refer to Chapter 2: Process Overview—Poppy Bloom (page 16).

MATERIALS

- **Print:** 21" × 22" for Outline Design
- **Variety of colors:** scraps (can be fashion fabrics)

- **Paper-backed fusible web** (such as Heat*n*Bond Lite): 2½ yards
- **Batting:** 23" × 24" of low loft
- **Backing:** 23" × 24"

- **Binding:** ¼ yard
- **Clear cellophane wrapping paper:** 1 yard
- **Vinyl:** for ¼"-strip stencil, scrap about 2" × 10"

MAKE THE FABRIC BACKGROUND

1. Create 1 sheet of the fusible web 21" × 22" by connecting 2 pieces with masking tape. Repeat to make a second sheet 23" × 24".

2. Fuse 1 large sheet of fusible web onto the batting, let it cool, and remove the paper backing.

3. Make a collage on the fused side of the batting using the scraps, placing the pieces rom edge to edge. Fill the entire piece of batting. Iron-baste each piece at 2 points, using a small crafter's iron or the tip of an iron. If you need to correct the placement of some of the pieces, just pull them up and position them correctly.

4. Check the layout; be sure you do not see the batting between the shapes.

5. Cover the collage with a Teflon, paper, or fabric pressing sheet and press to fuse.

Collage fused to batting

CREATE THE OUTLINE DESIGN PATTERN

1. Cover collage with cellophane paper and pin in the 4 corners.

2. Remove a ¼″ × 8″ strip from the vinyl to make a stencil to create the Outline Design pattern.

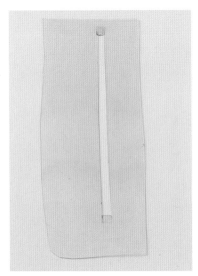

¼″-strip stencil from vinyl

3. Place the stencil on every fabric "seamline" (you will see the connections through the ¼″ stencil) and draw the ¼″-wide Outline Design lines. Draw a ¼″ frame around the Outline Design lines.

Create Outline Design pattern on cellophane.

Transfer design from cellophane in mirror image onto the fusible web.

Fabric for Outline Design

4. Write a letter R on the cellophane paper and turn it onto the wrong side.

5. Transfer the pattern in mirror image onto the paper backing of the fusible web.

CUT OUT THE OUTLINE DESIGN

1. Center the Outline Design on the wrong side of the print fabric. Fuse it by ironing on both the paper and fabric sides, following the manufacturer's directions. Check to make sure it fused across the entire piece. Let it cool.

2. Refer to Cutting Techniques (page 9) to cut out the design.

3. Gently remove the paper backing.

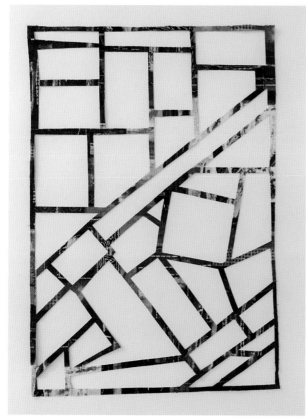

Outline Design cut from fabric

ADD THE OUTLINE DESIGN TO THE BACKGROUND

1. Place the Design Outline over the collage, check the layout to be sure all the background "seams" are covered with the Outline Design, and pin in the 4 corners.

2. Cover with a Teflon, paper, or fabric pressing sheet and press the entire quilt to fuse everything together.

FINISHING

1. See Finishing Raw Edges of Outline Designs (page 91). I used Method 2: Stitched Raw Edges (page 91). Use your favorite stitches, bits, buttons, and found objects to embellish your quilt.

Embroidery stitches

2. Layer, quilt (I used simple quilting on the outlines), square up the quilt, and bind.

ROSY BLOOM

FINISHED QUILT: 23¼″ × 23¼″

The Outline Design lines are thick and easy to cut and handle. The design is made up of simple geometric shapes repeated eight times in a circle design. Rather than making patterns from cellophane to cut the background fabrics, we will use the cutouts from the Outline Designer as patterns. I made this quilt for stained-glass window lovers. I used gradation fabrics, but you can choose prints, photos printed on fabric, or a combination.

Before starting your project, read Introduction (page 6) and Basic Instructions (page 89). For more detailed instructions, refer to Chapter 2: Process Overview—Poppy Bloom (page 16).

MATERIALS

- Black fabric (I used a batik): 24″ × 24″
- Green-yellow cotton: 1 fat quarter
- Lilac: 1 fat quarter
- Red: 1 fat quarter

- Blue: 1 fat quarter
- Yellow: 1 fat quarter
- Paper-backed fusible web (such as Heat*n*Bond Lite): 2⅞ yards

- Batting: 26″ × 26″ of low loft
- Backing: 26″ × 26″
- Binding: ¼ yard

CREATE THE OUTLINE DESIGN PATTERN

1. Create 1 sheet of the fusible web 24″ × 24″ by connecting 2 pieces with masking tape. Repeat to make a second sheet 26″ × 26″.

2. Trace the *Rosy Bloom* Outline Design pattern (page 65) onto the paper backing side of the fusible web.

3. Fuse the Outline Design onto the black fabric, following the manufacturer's instructions.

CUT OUT THE OUTLINE DESIGN

1. Center the Outline Design on the wrong side of the black fabric. Fuse it by ironing on both the paper and fabric sides, following the manufacturer's directions. Check to make sure it fused across the entire piece. Let it cool.

2. Refer to Cutting Techniques (page 9) to cut out the design. Save the cutouts to use as patterns for cutting out the background fabrics.

3. Remove the paper backing from the Outline Design.

ADD THE FABRIC BACKGROUND

1. Fuse the other piece of fusible web onto the batting, let it cool, and remove the paper backing.

2. Position the Outline Design on the fused side of the batting and pin in 4 corners.

3. Choose the fabrics you want to use for one section of the design. Pin the pattern cutout onto the appropriate fabric. Mark the cutting line ⅛" larger than the shape and cut on the line with scissors.

You can stack up to 4 layers of fabric for pinning and cutting out the background pieces.

4. Remove the paper backing and insert the shapes between the Outline Design and the batting, using tweezers, if necessary, and pin.

5. Repeat Steps 3 and 4 for every shape, one shape at a time. That way you will not be confused with where each shape and fabric goes.

6. Check to be sure all the pieces are aligned. Use tweezers to move the shapes under the Outline Design.

7. Set the iron on the Cotton or Wool setting and press using an up-and-down motion consistently over the whole quilt top. Let it cool.

FINISHING

1. See Finishing Raw Edges of Outline Designs (page 91). I used Method 1: Couched Raw Edges (page 91) using black metallic yarn.

2. Layer, quilt, square up the quilt, and bind.

Rosy Bloom color variation 1

Rosy Bloom color variation 2

Rosy Bloom color variation 3

Rosy Bloom Outline Design pattern (enlarge 350%)

SPACE NET

FINISHED QUILT: 22″ × 21″

This asymmetrical design is so interesting that it doesn't need the addition of extra background fabrics. A single gradated fabric placed in a different orientation for the Design Outline and background is enough. If you can't find a gradated fabric, use the curvy Flying Geese section as the dividing line to connect two different fabrics. Be creative and always try to imagine the final result. Cut swatches and see how they look together.

Before starting your project, read Introduction (page 6) and Basic Instructions (page 89). For more detailed instructions, refer to Chapter 2: Process Overview—Poppy Bloom (page 16).

MATERIALS

▪ Rainbow gradated fabric: 2 pieces 22″ × 21″

▪ Paper-backed fusible web (such as Heat*n*Bond Lite): 1¼ yards

▪ Batting: 24″ × 23″ of low loft

▪ Backing: 24″ × 23″

▪ Binding: ¼ yard

▪ Very thin, navy blue tulle (optional): 24″ × 23″

Rainbow gradated fabric

CREATE THE OUTLINE DESIGN PATTERN

1. Create 1 sheet of the fusible web 22″ × 21″ by connecting 2 pieces with masking tape.

2. Trace the *Space Net* Outline Design pattern (page 69) onto the paper backing side of the fusible web.

3. Fuse the Outline Design onto one of the rainbow gradated fabrics, following the manufacturer's instructions.

CUT OUT THE OUTLINE DESIGN

1. Center the Outline Design on the wrong side of the other rainbow gradated fabric. Fuse it by ironing on both the paper and fabric sides, following the manufacturer's directions. Check to make sure it fused across the entire piece. Let it cool.

2. Refer to Cutting Technniques (page 9) to cut out the design. Use scissors to cut any areas that are challenging with the craft knife.

3. Remove the paper backing.

>
>
> If you want to make a second quilt later, save the cutouts and gently remove the paper backing from the Outline Design to position the pieces onto the background fabric (see *Butterfly Garden* Note, page 27).

ADD THE FABRIC BACKGROUND

1. Position the second piece of rainbow fabric so that the colors of the Outline Design and background don't line up. Rotate the background piece, if necessary.

2. Set the iron on the Cotton or Wool setting and press using an up-and-down motion consistently over the whole quilt top.

Fabric rotated for contrast

FINISHING

1. See Finishing Raw Edges of Outline Designs (page 91). I used Method 3: Tulle-Covered Design (page 92).

2. Layer, quilt, square up the quilt, and bind.

Space Net color variation

Space Net Outline Design pattern (enlarge 300%)

Inspiration THREEPLIQUÉ

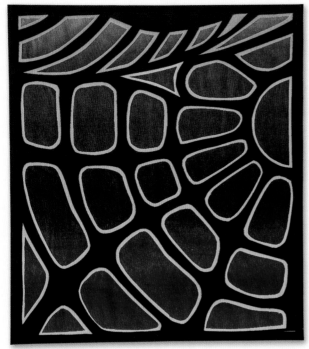

Threepliqué—sample 1

Threepliqué—sample 3

Threepliqué—sample 2

I called this style *Threepliqué*. For sample 1, I made one Outline Design in black fabric and cut it out. Next, I fused paper-backed fusible web onto the yellow-orange fabric, and before removing the paper backing, I fused the black Outline Design on top of the yellow-orange fabric. I removed the paper backing from the yellow-orange fabric and cut the secondary echo shapes on the right side of the fabric ⅛˝ inside the black fabric edges. I chose purple-blue gradation for the background to contrast with the yellow orange. It looks attractive and neat and can be used for all the projects.

Sample 2 is created from three gradation-colored fabrics in complementary colors. The thin secondary lines complement the design—dark on light and light on dark.

The Outline Design of sample 3 is cut from a bright print and the secondary outline is cut from black batik and fused onto the gradated green background.

To finish the raw edges of all Threepliqué quilts, I recommend that you cover the fused quilt top with tulle (see Method 3: Tulle-Covered Design, page 92) and use the quilting of your choice.

Well, cats like to get what they want, when nobody is watching! You should see their innocent eyes after every attempt: "It wasn't me."

Try using the Outline Design technique to make a pictorial quilt. You can make an Outline Design pattern from a photograph (see Option 6: Using Photographs, page 87).

In this particular project, I painted the cat and fishbowl fabric, but you can also print images onto sheets of HeatnBond EZ-Print Lite. If you have dogs, cats, roosters, horses, cows, goats, or something else, now you can make pictorial quilts with their faces and in their environment. Of course you can also make the image by using separate fabrics to fill the Outline Design openings.

Color variation

Level-Three Quilt Projects

KOI POND

CHAPTER 5

FINISHED QUILT: 22½″ × 22″

Koi Pond *was created as a sample of an organic* Outline Design *on a solid gradated background. I thought everyone would enjoy finding the hidden interpretation of the subject in this design. Some ideas are fire and water, male and female, shadow and light, positive and negative—complimentary forces in different dualities that you can interpret as you think about it. I drew the fish like yin and yang, but it is up to you what you can see in it.*

Before starting your project, read Introduction (page 6) and Basic Instructions (page 89). For more detailed instructions, refer to Chapter 2: Process Overview—Poppy Bloom (page 16).

MATERIALS

- Black fabric (I used black batik): 22½″ × 22″

- Gradation fabric: 23″ × 23″ for background

- Theatrical fabrics: 1 fat quarter each of emerald green, white holographic, 2 different

- multicolored holographics, and red (*optional*), and 10″ × 10″ of yellow green

- Paper-backed fusible web (such as Heat*n*Bond Lite): 3⅝ yards

- Batting: 25″ × 25″ of low loft

- Backing: 25″ × 25″

- Binding: ¼ yard

- Clear cellophane wrapping paper: 1 yard

- Very thin, navy blue tulle (optional): 22″ × 22″

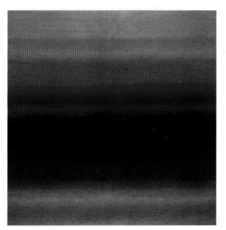

Background fabric

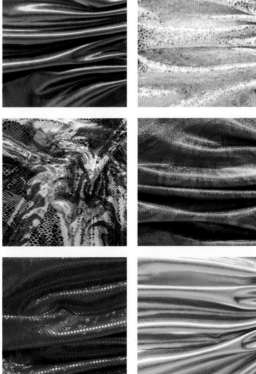

Theatrical fabrics

CREATE THE OUTLINE DESIGN PATTERN

1. Create 1 sheet of the fusible web 22½″ × 22″ by connecting 2 pieces with masking tape.

2. Trace the *Koi Pond* Outline Design pattern onto the paper backing of the fusible web.

3. Fuse the Outline Design onto the black fabric, following the manufacturer's instructions.

CUT OUT THE OUTLINE DESIGN

1. Center the Outline Design on the wrong side of the black fabric. Fuse it by ironing on both the paper and fabric sides, following the manufacturer's directions. Check to make sure it fused across the entire piece. Let it cool.

2. Refer to Cutting Techniques (page 9) to cut out the design. Cut out the smallest parts first. Place the cutouts into a plastic bag if you plan to use them for a second project (see *Butterfly Garden*, page 25, and *Night Butterfly*, page 29).

3. Remove the paper backing from the Outline Design.

ADD THE FABRIC BACKGROUND

1. Layer the backing fabric, batting, and the background fabrics; spray with basting spray (see Basting the Quilt Layers, page 90). Let it dry and iron on both sides.

2. Carefully iron the fusible web to the wrong side of the theatrical fabrics with an iron set on Wool. These fabrics are very heat sensitive, so be sure to use a Teflon, paper, or fabric pressing sheet.

3. Place the Outline Design onto the quilt sandwich, straighten it, and pin it on the 4 corners.

4. One by one, trace the koi fish, fish fins, lily, and leaves from the design onto the cellophane paper ⅛″ bigger around than the shape you see (in the windows), using a black fine-point permanent marker. The marker line will be in the middle of the design lines.

5. Cut the pieces from the cellophane a little bigger than the drawn line, one at a time. Write the letter R on the cellophane. Place it on the right side of the chosen fabrics and pin.

6. Cut out the pieces on the marked line and remove the paper.

7. Insert the pieces under the Outline Design, using tweezers, if necessary.

8. Pin the shapes in place using only thin metal pins (no plastic). Later you will press the quilt top over the pins.

9. Check to be sure that all the pieces are aligned. Use tweezers to move the shapes under the Outline Design.

10. Set the iron on the Wool setting and press with an up-and-down motion consistently over the whole quilt top using a Teflon, paper, or fabric pressing sheet. Let it cool. Take your time, and check to be sure the elements are fused; remove the pins as you go.

FINISHING

1. See Finishing Raw Edges of Outline Designs (page 91). I used Method 3: Tulle-Covered Design (page 92).

2. Quilt, square up the quilt, and bind.

Koi Pond Outline Design pattern (enlarge 300%)

DESERT FLOWER

FINISHED QUILT: 21½″ × 21½″

This quilt has a traditional and complicated look, but it's easy to make. The Outline Design lines are wider than in most of the other projects. This quilt uses a monochromatic color scheme in four shades of orange. You can use four shades of any color or a wider color gradation.

Before starting your project, read Introduction (page 6) and Basic Instructions (page 89). For more detailed instructions, refer to Chapter 2: Process Overview— Poppy Bloom (page 16).

MATERIALS

- **Black fabric (I used a batik):** 21½″ × 21½″

- **Orange fabrics:** 1 fat quarter each of 4 shades: light, medium light, medium dark, and dark

- **Paper-backed fusible web (such as Heat*n*Bond Lite):** 2⅛ yards

- **Batting:** 26″ × 26″ of low loft

- **Backing:** 26″ × 26″

- **Binding:** ¼ yard

- **Clear cellophane wrapping paper:** 1 yard

- **Swarovski crystals (optional):** for embellishment

CREATE THE OUTLINE DESIGN PATTERN

1. Create 1 sheet of the fusible web 21½″ × 21½″ by connecting 2 pieces with masking tape. Repeat to make a second sheet 26″ × 26″.

2. Trace the ¼ of the *Desert Flower* Outline Design pattern (page 79) onto the paper backing side of the smaller sheet of fusible web. You will need to trace the pattern 4 times (rotating as necessary) to create the entire design.

3. Fuse the Outline Design onto the black fabric, following the manufacturer's instructions.

CUT OUT THE OUTLINE DESIGN

1. Center the Outline Design on the wrong side of the black fabric. Fuse it by ironing on both the paper and fabric sides, following the manufacturer's directions. Check to make sure it fused across the entire piece. Let it cool.

2. Refer to Cutting Techniques (page 9) to cut out the design.

3. Remove the paper backing.

ADD THE FABRIC BACKGROUND

1. Fuse the other piece of fusible web onto the batting, let it cool, and remove the paper backing.

2. Position the Outline Design on the fused side of the batting and pin in the 4 corners.

3. Choose the sections of the design you want to include on each fabric (including the small appliqués). Trace each section onto the cellophane paper separately, one at a time, ⅛″ bigger around than the shape you see (in the windows), using a black fine-point permanent marker. The marker line will be in the middle of the design lines.

4. Cut the pieces from the cellophane a little bigger than the drawn line, one at the time. Write the letter R on the cellophane. Place it on the right side of the colorful fabric and pin.

5. Cut out the shapes on the marked line and insert them between the Outline Design and the batting, using tweezers if necessary, and pin.

6. Iron-baste each piece, using a small crafter's iron or the tip of an iron, on 2 points as you insert them. Try not to touch the Outline Design dividing strips with the iron at this stage or it will stick before you're ready. If you need to correct the placement of some of the pieces, just pull them up and position them correctly.

7. Check to be sure all the pieces are aligned. Use tweezers to move the shapes under the Outline Design.

8. Set the iron on the Cotton or Wool setting and press using an up-and-down motion consistently over the whole quilt top. Let it cool.

9. Add small extra pieces of fused-fabric details to the background as appliquéd embellishments, if you wish.

FINISHING

1. See Finishing Raw Edges of Outline Designs (page 91). I used Method 1: Couched Raw Edges (page 91).

2. Layer, quilt, square up the quilt, and bind.

Color variation 1 (shown in ¼ of design)

Color variation 2 (shown in ¼ of design)

Color variation 3 (shown in ¼ of design)

¼ of *Desert Flower* Outline Design pattern (enlarge 150%)

Desert Flower Outline Design pattern

Funky Reef is a good sample of organic, abstract art. I spontaneously drew the design elements, which slightly remind me of seashells, water creatures, and seaweed. The bright colors celebrate life and happiness and bring back memories. The variety of size of the elements is very important. Sometimes the larger ones compliment the small ones and vice versa. I turned and twisted, moved, changed the size, and shaped them to fit together. The variety of elements combine into one complete composition.

I couched the raw edges with black metallic yarn and embellished areas with black hot-fix Swarovski crystals. I quilted the black Outline Design with microstippling and bubble quilted the colored shapes.

Detail of quilting

This quilt was inspired by the architectural structure, carved details, windows, and paintings on antique churches and cathedrals in Portugal, Spain, and France. I took photographs and drew sketches and created a collage on paper for the center star. I scanned the design and processed it through Kaleidoscope Kreator 3 (kalcollections.com), my favorite computer program. I printed the pattern on multiple pages using the poster feature. In certain places I had to leave small strips uncut to prevent the design from falling apart. I airbrushed the center of the star, using light-brown paint, in a circular motion to create a gradation effect.

The background squares and triangles were made separately from scraps and small pieces of commercial and painted fabric. Then I added embroidery, couching with metallic yarn, black Swarovski crystals, and hot-fix pearls.

The quilting was done using multiple microstippling to fill the white parts of the star; for the architectural parts I quilted on the stenciled and embroidered design lines. The black Outline Design on white organizes the whole composition.

CHAPTER 6

Designing Your Own Outline-Design Quilt

CHOOSING COLORS

Audition different background colors to find just the perfect one(s).

Make multiple copies of the Outline Design pattern on regular 8½″ × 11″ printing paper. Using colored pencils or markers, fill in the design with different colors. Don't forget to use light on dark and dark on light.

Another option is to use the color scheme of your favorite fabric print, which usually is printed on one of the selvages.

Here are a few color palettes I created for *Diamond Cut* (page 21).

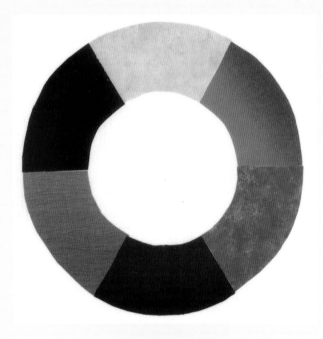

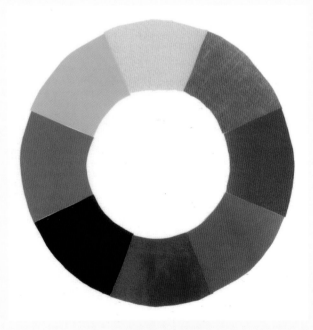

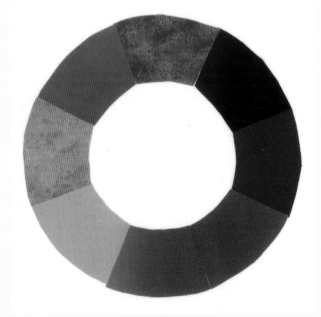

DESIGN INSPIRATION POSSIBILITIES

When you create your Outline Design pattern, you need to keep a few things in mind:

- Make sure the width of the lines is wide enough to cut out easily and hide the raw edges of your background fabrics.

- Your design lines need to softly flow from one to another.

- Make a ¼"-wide temporary frame around the entire outside edge and add connecting lines between the elements to hold the design together so that it remains in one piece after you cut out your Design Outline.

OPTION 1 *Using an Existing Image*

When you're ready to create your own original Outline Design quilts, you can find inspiration in lots of places, including royalty-free images and coloring books.

Outline Design pattern based on this drawing

OPTION 2 *Using a Doodle or Freehand Drawing*

Make a ¼"-wide temporary frame around the entire outside edge of your design area. With a black marker, doodle or freehand draw spontaneous lines, filling the space with curvy lines that cross back and forth; enjoy the freedom. When you think it is enough, you can add some simple organic or geometric shapes, circles, and free-form elements if you want to. Thicken the design lines and add the connecting lines and additional shapes to add interest. Look at the design and modify any areas that don't look balanced. You can use correction fluid to cover unwanted parts.

Doodle drawing

Outline Design from the doodle drawing

OPTION 3 *Using Kaleidoscope Kreator 3*

You can continue to modify your Outline Design pattern by processing it through Kaleidoscope Kreator 3 (kalcollections.com). Scan the Outline Design pattern into your computer and make different mandala images from your design using the program instructions. When you have a design you like, print the design on multiple pages, using poster printing in a photo-editing program such as Photoshop. You can usually find the poster printing option under Options in Printer Properties. Use white glue to connect pages and you will have the full-size Outline Design pattern ready to trace onto paper-backed fusible web.

Kaleidoscope designs made from doodle outlines drawn in Option 2 (page 83)

OPTION 4 *Using a Traditional Quilt Block Design*

With a black marker, draw geometric or organic shapes; they do not have to be symmetrical. Use tools and rulers or draw freehand.

You can turn your favorite quilting block into an Outline Design pattern. Use it alone or repeat it a few times and make the quilt look traditional with an artistic twist of blocks. You can make freehand curvy lines for the block using an extra-thick marker.

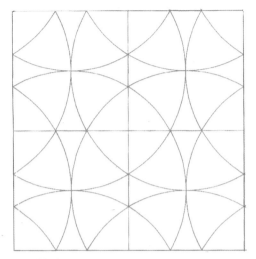

Quilt block

Freehand curvy Log Cabin Outline Design pattern

Modified drawing in progress

Curvy Log Cabin outline in color

Quilt Outline Design pattern from block

OPTION 5 *Using Found Objects*

Outline your favorite objects, like tree leaves, in a variety of shapes and sizes. Overlap them and create a frame to connect the design. You can use real fresh leaves, grass, or flattened flowers to name a few possibilities. Stencils are a good source of shapes and elements to use for this technique if you are not an experienced artist. Any size of shapes and elements can be used to create the design to be enlarged later.

Outline Design pattern using tree leaves

Tree leaves

Fabric for Outline Design

Sketch of leaves for Outline Design pattern

Outline Design in fabric

Use photographs of still lifes, landscapes, seascapes, your favorite pets, birds, wild animals, people, and even portraits. *City Scape* (page 37) is an example of this option.

Here are two ways to do it:

- Enlarge the photo to the size of the quilt you want to make plus a ½" frame around the edges. In this stage you can print it in multiple pages in black and white and connect them together. This is a map to make the outline. Cover the image with clear cellophane wrapping paper (you can connect a few pieces together with clear tape). Outline the main shapes and elements of the image in the photo using a black marker; your drawing lines should divide shades and light changes, borders of color change, separate shapes, forms, and elements. Connect the elements to each other and to the drawn frame. Add the details and connect them with other designs, adding any other elements you need to balance the composition; use the different width of your lines and be creative.

- Cover the original-size picture with clear cellophane wrapping paper and draw the outline using a fine-point marker. Fill in the appropriate areas with a marker. When you finish the small Outline Design pattern, scan it and enlarge it by printing a poster-size copy or using a print shop.

Example photo

Black-and-white photo

Outline Design pattern on clear cellophane

Example photo

Black-and-white photo

Outline Design pattern on cellophane

OPTION 7 *Using a Computer Drawing Program*

You can use a paint program from the accessories folder in your computer and make an abstract design with straight, continuous lines from point to point or freehand continuous lines. Or, you can create mandalas without a special program. Any shape, abstract or representational (animals, birds, flowers, trees, fish), can be your inspiration; even your own quilts can be your inspiration or part of your Outline Design patterns.

1. Draw a design.

2. Print the drawing on a piece of 8½" × 11" paper.

3. Draw a medium-size right isosceles triangle (having one 90° angle and two 45° angles) on a second piece of paper and cut it out.

Sample outline made from drawing

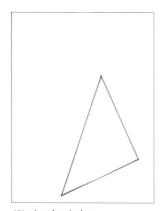

45° triangle window

4. Place the triangle on top of the design and move it around, until you see an interesting design inside the triangle. With the triangle paper over the design area you like, make a photocopy and a mirror-image photocopy.

Design in triangle

5. Cut out both triangles and put them together to connect the design lines.

Mirror image designs

6. Make 4 photocopies. Cut and connect them, make a photocopy, and you will have your Outline Design pattern.

Printed copy of design—variation 1

Printed copy of design—variation 2

7. Enlarge the design to the size you want your quilt to be. Trace it onto the appropriate size of paper-backed fusible web.

You can make mandalas from 4, 6, 8, 12, 16, and more different sizes of wedges. They can be made using mirror images of every 2 wedges or in the pinwheel order.

Basic Instructions

CHAPTER 7

ALTERNATIVE METHOD FOR CREATING THE OUTLINE DESIGN PATTERN

Rather than tracing the pattern onto the paper side of fusible web, using a computer and printer, you can copy and print the pattern on multiple pages, like a poster, onto Heat*n*Bond EZ-Print Lite 20 precut sheets. These individual sheets can then be positioned and fused onto fabric to create the Outline Design.

MAKING A DESIGNING BOARD

You can use this board for ironing, designing, pinning, and more. It is great for quilting classes, carries easily in the car, and stores neatly behind a door.

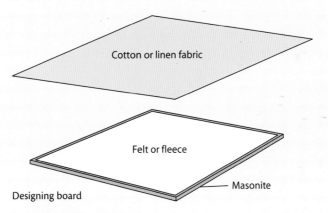

Cotton or linen fabric

Felt or fleece

Masonite

Designing board

MATERIALS

- Heavyweight cotton fabric: 28″ × 28″ for front cover and 23″ × 23″ for backing
- Masonite board: 24″ × 24″ × ⅛″

- Fleece, felt, or medium-loft batting: 24″ × 24″
- White school glue

tip

Ask the lumberyard to cut the Masonite for you.

CONSTRUCTION

1. On one side of the Masonite, apply the glue in wavy lines, 2″ apart, in a grid pattern.

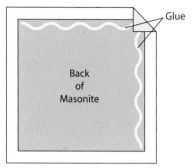

Apply glue to one side of Masonite.

2. Center the fleece or felt on top of the glued side.

3. Turn the board upside down and center it onto the wrong side of the bigger piece of heavyweight cotton fabric.

4. Squeeze a small amount of glue on each corner, covering 2″ × 2″ spaces, and fold the corners of the fabric over each corner, one by one.

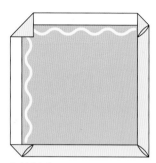

Fold fabric over corners.

Back fabric cover

Put small amount of glue on raw edges of sides and flip them to connect with the board surface.

5. Center the other piece of heavy-weight cotton fabric on the other side of the Masonite.

6. Fold one half of the fabric over, so it is on top of the other half of the fabric, right sides together.

7. Apply glue around the edge, on the half of the fabric that is now wrong side up, about ¼″ from the raw edges, and add glue on the Masonite. Unfold the glued half and attach it onto the board.

8. Repeat Step 7 for the remaining half of the fabric.

9. Smooth the fabric and let the glue dry.

BASTING THE QUILT LAYERS

The best way to baste the quilt sandwich together is to use quilter's basting spray. This spray will temporarily hold the layers together while the quilting is being done.

tip

1. Place the ironed backing fabric, right side up. onto the batting.

2. Fold one half of the backing over, so it is on top of the other half of the backing, right sides together; you will see only half of the batting and half of the wrong side of the backing.

3. Spray the basting spray over half of the wrong side of the backing. Be sure to protect the surface around your quilt and follow the manufacturer's instructions.

4. Using both hands, open the sprayed half of the backing and gently smooth it onto the batting, stretching it gently.

   If your quilt is large, do this on the floor by holding and stretching the back-ground by the corners and walking backward on top of your quilt, until you match the corners.

FINISHING RAW EDGES OF OUTLINE DESIGNS

NOTE

You should leave the raw edges unfinished only if you are adding very close lines of quilting that cover the entire design and will prevent any fraying.

Microstippling

METHOD 1 Couched Raw Edges

My favorite way to finish the raw edges of my quilts is with couching. When the background Outline Design shapes are filled with colored fabrics and everything is fused to the batting, it's time to cover all the raw edges of your quilt top. Couching is a technique to zigzag yarn or embroidery threads onto the fabric. Usually I use the metallic yarn and 100% nylon clear invisible .004 mm thread. After everything is couched, hide the ends of the yarn on the batting side, using a big needle. Attach the backing fabric and quilt through all the layers.

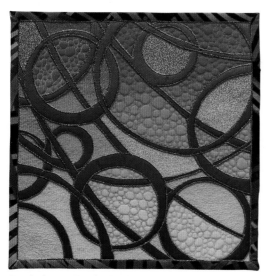

Couched raw edges (quilted)

METHOD 2 Stitched Raw Edges

A simple and traditional method to cover the raw edges is to use a satin stitch, a tiny zigzag, or an invisible appliqué stitch.

Satin-stitched raw edges

Another way to cover the raw edges is to use decorative embroidery stitches. Use this method with the quilt top attached to the batting, but before the backing fabric is added.

Decorative stitches on *Lazy-Crazy* (page 58)

METHOD 3 *Tulle-Covered Design*

Another possibility is to make a quilt sandwich, attaching a prewashed and ironed backing with basting spray (page 90).

Cover the entire quilt top with thin, fine navy blue tulle. This will not change the fabric colors on your quilt. Pin it evenly across the surface and stitch, following the design lines.

Tulle-covered design

 tip

Tulle is a two-way stretch fabric, but it stretches less on the grain, so stitch on the grain first, if the design will allow you to. Or, starting from the center and working toward the sides, stitch using your favorite quilting designs.

 NOTE

Tulle is very heat sensitive, so iron or steam the finished quilt from the back side or use a Teflon, fabric, or paper pressing sheet.

EMBELLISHMENTS

Couching on *Butterfly Dance* (full quilt, page 32)

Swarovski crystals on *Funky Reef* (full quilt, page 80)

Heat-set sequins on *Cathedral Star* (full quilt, page 81)

Embroidery stitches on *Cathedral Star* (full quilt, page 81)

DOUBLE-FOLD STRAIGHT-GRAIN BINDING (FRENCH FOLD)

1. Trim excess batting and backing from the quilt. If you want a ¼" finished binding, cut the binding strips 2¼" wide and piece them together with diagonal seams to make a continuous binding strip. Trim the seam allowances and press the seams open.

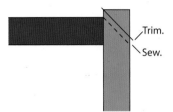

Stitch diagonal seams and trim.

Press open.

2. Press the entire strip in half lengthwise with wrong sides together and raw edges even.

3. Align the raw edges of the binding with the raw edges of the quilt top. Pin the binding to the edge of the quilt, starting a few inches away from a corner. Leave the first several inches of the binding unattached. Start sewing, using a ¼" seam allowance.

4. Stop ¼" from the first corner and backstitch one stitch.

Stop stitching ¼" from the first corner.

5. Lift the presser foot and needle. Rotate the quilt one-quarter turn. Fold the binding at a 45° angle, so that it extends straight above the quilt.

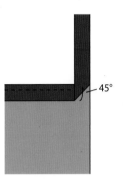

First fold for miter

6. Fold the binding strip down, even with the top and side edges of the quilt. Begin sewing at the folded edge.

Second fold alignment

7. Repeat in the same manner at the remaining corners.

FINISHING THE BINDING

Choose between these two methods for finishing the binding.

METHOD 1

1. Open the end of the binding strip and fold it under ¼". Press.

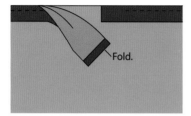

Fold binding end under ¼".

2. Refold the strip on its original lengthwise fold to get a finished edge on this end of the binding strip.

3. Place the beginning binding strip on top of the ending strip that has the folded edge.

4. Trim the excess from the beginning binding strip about ½" beyond the folded edge of the ending strip.

5. Continue stitching the overlapped binding strips to the quilt.

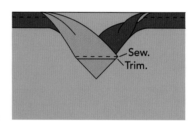

Overlap strips and complete seam.

6. Fold the binding over the raw edges to the quilt back and hand stitch the binding to the back, mitering the corners.

METHOD 2

1. Fold the ending tail of the binding back on itself where it meets the beginning tail.

2. From the fold, measure and mark the cut width of the binding strip. Cut the ending binding tail to this measurement. For example, if your binding strip is cut 2½" wide, measure this amount from the fold on the ending binding tail and cut the binding tail to this length.

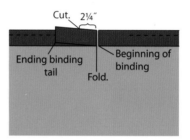

Fold and then cut binding tail to cut width of binding.

3. Open both tails. Place tail on top of the other tail at right angles, right sides together. Mark a diagonal line and stitch on the line. Trim the seam allowance to ¼". Press the seam open.

Stitch ends of binding diagonally.

4. Refold the binding on its original lengthwise fold and finish sewing the binding to the quilt.

5. Fold the binding over the raw edges to the quilt back and hand stitch the binding to the back, mitering the corners.

Visit us at **ctpub.com**
and receive a special offer

For inspiring content that keeps you smiling and sewing

Find out what's new
at C&T PUBLISHING

FREE Projects ▪ FREE How-to Videos

Blog ▪ Books ▪ Patterns ▪ Tools ▪ Rulers

Templates ▪ TAP Transfer Artist Paper

kraft•tex™ ▪ & more

Go to
ctpub.com/offer

*Sign up and receive
your special offer*

About the Author

Anna Faustino was born in St. Petersburg, Russia. The stars must have been smiling that day because an artist was born.

Making dresses for her dolls led to making her own clothes and embellishing the costumes of the performers at the Kirov Theatre (now known as the Mariinsky Theatre). Anna has always enjoyed creating beautiful things.

After immigrating to the United States, Anna discovered the world of quilting, and her imagination went wild. Beginning with some basic designs, she quickly started experimenting with her own designs and techniques, leading her to write her first book, *Simply Stunning Woven Quilts*. The colorful art quilts she creates are truly works to admire and to inspire quilters to think outside the box and see that there are no limits to what one can do with fabrics. This book is a testament to the possibilities of creativity in art and discovering different and exciting quilting techniques.

Also by Anna Faustino:

Available as Print-on-Demand only